My Road Trip To Heaven

The Supernatural Works of God

Dr. Alva Wilson

Copyright © 2015 by Dr. Alva Wilson

My Road Trip To Heaven
The Supernatural Works of God
by Dr. Alva Wilson

Printed in the United States of America.

ISBN 9781498437301

All rights reserved solely by the author. The author guarantees all contents are original and do not infringe upon the legal rights of any other person or work. No part of this book may be reproduced in any form without the permission of the author. The views expressed in this book are not necessarily those of the publisher.

Unless otherwise indicated, Scripture quotations taken from the King James Version (KJV) Copyright © 2012 by Morris Cerullo World Evangelism. Used by permission of Tyndale House Publishers, Inc.

www.xulonpress.com

My Personal Introduction for Speaking Engagements

*S*ister Alva R. Oliver Wilson, a native of Harrison Switch and Waco, Texas. I was closely connected to the people of Bosqueville, Texas and its church members. I was especially connected to the beloved Pastor and his brothers, the Montgomery Family. Why? Because my dad was their pastor. Therefore while growing up, Alva Ree Oliver was in Bosqueville Baptist Church, as often as the doors swung open. While there I served as Sunday School Secretary, sang in the Choir with Sister Christina Bradshaw Montgomery, the well known and well loved musician.

I attended Paul Quinn College — united in Holy Matrimony in 1961 — moved away. After an unfortunate divorce, "I was hurting so much, I was desperate for God's intervention in my life. That's when He called me to preach — I said, 'Yes, my Lord' and my life has never been the same."

I was a military wife for 12 years and mother of 3 grown children, Jackie (Todd) Cranford both are attorney's in Washington, D.C.; Clarence (Debbie) Wilson, he's a computer analyst; and baby boy, Tony, a truck driver residing in Columbia, S.C. I have six grandchildren and 3 great grand's.

I, Evangelist Wilson, hold a BA Degree — that is, A Born Again Degree in Christianity and a B.S. Degree in Drug and Alcohol Abuse Counseling and I have attained a Doctorate Degree in Missionary Work.

Evangelist Wilson has traveled extensively world wide — traveling to Germany, Mexico, England, Norway and most recently Israel to the Holy Land several times. I have walked where Jesus walked and was baptized in the Jordan River.

Alva, a poet, song writer, and the author of <u>From Victim to Victory</u>, a book about Sexual Abuse Beyond Belief. <u>From Victim To Victory</u> tells you how to protect a child from abuse and how to get delivered. My latest book is still listed on Amazon.com and also on Barnes & Noble. My Road Trip To Heaven, a supernatural work of God, should be coming out mid-summer 2015.

Presently she is an Elder under the leadership of Dr. Morris Cerullo's World Evangelistic Association (MCWE). Most of all Alva says, "I am a friend of God and God's people. I'm in Love with Jesus."

Preface

The Word of the Lord had already spoken to me concerning the supernatural Work that He had planned for me, and for All those who are obedient to His word. This Prophetic Word of the Lord was confirmed here by Prophet Dr. Morris Cerullo. Dr. Cerullo said:

> *"Alva, God has shown me that I am to release a supernatural anointing personally to my Partners. The moment I release this anointing, God is going to manifest an overflow of His blessings that will be your miraculous provision for the rest of your life!!!"*
>
> *God's Servant,*
> *Morris Cerullo*

> *ps: "Alva, our anointing service at this World Conference will be the most amazing that we have ever conducted. I will be anointing you for a specific purpose: That God will give you the gift of supernatural eyesight, that you will see God's VISION for your life, and that you will*

fulfill your DIVINE DESTINY. Come, receive your SUPERNATURAL ANOINTING!!!

My Lord had already spoken to me about the Supernatural eyesight and work that He has planned for me, and for All those who are obedient to His word. Dr. Cerullo confirmed it, by the prophetic words written above.

Acknowledgments:

Thanks to...

The Father, Son, and Holy Spirit who has dictated and directed me to write this second book.

In Honor and Recognition of

First Lady Loretta Hartfield Oliver

Greater New Light Missionary Baptist Church of Waco, Texas

Thank you for your time and labor of love transforming this book. You are a kind, gentle and loving spirit, a super-busy wife, mother, grand-mother, and first lady of a large congregation. While working in the church office and keeping an eye on all those people, one would wonder "how can she do all this while serving on a hospital board and other positions?" It's Supernatural! Thank you mighty woman of God!

Special Thanks To

Co-Pastor Cynthia Jones! You were helpful to me in the compilation of gathering the required knowledge and skills to get this second book published. Thank you for your personal time and investment in this project. During the publication of my first book, From Victim To Victory you devoted your time (edited and assisted with cover design) to that book as well, considering the many hats that you wore. Thanks again for your Labor of Love!

Table of Contents

Preface..vii
Acknowledgments....................................ix
Definitions.......................................xiii
My Prayer For You..................................xv
Dedicated To.....................................xvii
Introduction......................................xix
The Greatest Supernatural Work....................xxi
Chapter I.   A Highway to Heaven................27
Chapter II.   Changing Drivers...................31
Chapter III.   During the Big Bang
                No Entrance — Do Not Enter.........35
Chapter IV.   No Fear Here.......................39
Chapter V.   Who Controlled and Stopped the Van?...41
Chapter VI.   The Flaming Torch..................43
Chapter VII.   The Two Intercessors
                God's Super Natural Intervention
                Sovereign Power....................45
Chapter VIII   The State Trooper Investigates.....49
Chapter IX.   Obedience–The Only Way to Go.......53
Chapter X.   Satan's Ploy to Destroy Me Uncovered...55
Chapter XI.   Back to School.....................61
Chapter XII.   Where Is Tony?.....................65
Chapter XIII.   What Happened With Mama?...........67
Chapter XIV.   The Long Journey to Complete Healing....71
Chapter XV.   The Miracle of Moving..............73

Definitions

Supernatural: *Beyond the observable physical world.*
Natural: *Not artificial — life like.*
Super: *In status or position.*
          [Meriam Webster Concise Dictionary]

My Prayer For You

Holy Spirit

Take us

Above

and

Beyond

Give us Supernatural Eyesight
Higher Than We've Ever Been Before

For God see's beyond our circumstances and beyond the actual and factual into the Supernatural!

Dedicated To

In Precious Memory
Of
Mama, Ann E. Oliver
Her Siblings & Spouse
Children, Grand Children & Generations to come

Also to
Minister Janie Fulmer who was accompanying
me on that L-I-F-E Changing Day

Introduction

While attending Indiana Wesleyan University, studying and working toward my degree as an Alcohol & Drug Abuse Counselor, students were released for break time, Summer semester session.

Evangelist Janie Fulmer and I decided to drive to Los Angeles, California. While there, we would volunteer our time for a very worthy cause. We would give one week's time at a ministry that Pastor Tommy Barnett and son had recently opened.

It was there, I would earn credit hours toward my degree. We thought this would be, not just a good idea; But a God idea. However, our trip was interrupted by a devastating, severely serious car accident. A death experience. That trip was never completed as planned. Consequently, we were detoured and took another route, which was "My Super Natural Road Trip to Heaven". Oh, what an adventure; to end-up standing at the "Pearlie Gates of Heaven" instead of working with the homeless, needy girls and women at the center in Los Angeles.

God had a better plan for me. Instead of a testimony concerning the center and the homeless women there, my story reflects the Glory of God, and what going to Heaven and back to Earth would be like for me.

Why write this book? To give Glory to God, and to share my Supernatural experience with you.

Janie Fulmer

To Be Absent From The Body.....

Who was Janie? She was a seer, a prophetess. She did not like to use titles. Everyone knew her as …..just Janie. She was known and loved by many as "just Janie"–not Miss or Mrs. or Prophetess or Evangelist. She was a mighty woman of faith who really really loved God and His people.

She is presently in Heaven in the presence of our Lord and Savior Jesus Christ. I can imagine her standing and looking over the beautiful Sapphire Seals of Glory; praying for her friend and teaching partner in ministry, Sister Alva (me), as well as others, to make it over there. I can also imagine that she is praying for the compilation and distribution of this book.

She had a tremendous love for the prophetic word and for the prophetess and prophet who carried and decreed the word. She guarded and held on to every prophetic word given to her. This dynamic, anointed seer was riding in the back of her luxury van when the accident happened. To be exact, she was lying down. The van was equipped with a bed, among other amenities. It was very cozy and comfortable for traveling. After driving the entire night while I rested, she finally had the chance to sleep.

As you will see later in this story, in Chapter II., we did not stop at the exact scene of the accident, but continued rolling and wobbling uncontrollable down Interstate 40 until we were supernaturally catapulted off the Interstate and into this roadside park. It was at the roadside park where God showed the state trooper His Supernatural Power. Did he believe it was God? The troopers started to question me about how the accident happened. I was out of my mind and talking nonsense. Janie spoke up and said "no Alva, that is not the way it happened". She proceeded to tell the state trooper what happened until he yelled at her "shut up woman, you were in the back seat sleep. How would you know?". Janie responded to him by saying "I just know!" She was highly insulted. The state trooper said "that's okay, we will find out. We are going back to the scene of the accident. We will ask the men there. They will know.".

The state troopers went back to the place of the accident to question the men there. They then returned to the roadside park where we were waiting. They came over and acknowledged that Janie had given very accurate information. One trooper asked, "how did you know this when you were in the back seat of the van sleeping?" Janie replied again, "I just know"!

Janie and I both knew that she was a seer/prophetess and that ultimately, God had shown her everything that transpired. That's how she knew. Consequently, she did not try to explain to the state troopers. They would not have understood. It's Supernatural.

After the excitement of the Supernatural life and death experience, and when the dust settled, that's when Janie began to look back and reflect on what had happened. She said to me, "Sister Alva, you need to write a book about our Supernatural experience!" My thought was "why don't you write the story?". At that time, I had never written a book.

Although I had taken a course in Journalism while in college, I didn't know how to start or where to start. Consequently, the thought of writing this story never left my mind!

Finally, sometime later (as spoken of in Chapter 1), I met Bob on an airplane and he also wanted to know if I had written my testimony. As I replied no, he asked me "why not?".

The Greatest Supernatural Work

There is a greater supernatural move on the horizon, yet to come, and I believe this will be the greatest move of God in the New Testament History of this kind.

THE FULFILLMENT of I Thessalonians 4:17-18 which says, "17 Then we who are alive and remain shall be caught up together with Him in the clouds to meet the Lord in the air, and so shall we always be with the Lord. 18 Therefore, comfort one another with these words." [New American Standard]

The greatest miracle of this category in the Old Testament time was the parting of the Red Sea, where He (God) Super Naturally parted the Red Sea and thousands of God's chosen children — the Jews — were freed from Slavery. The Israelites were free of bondage after years of involuntary servitude.

By this Bible story alone, you can see that we live in two different worlds. The natural world; the only world that most people know about; and the Super Natural world, the world that can only be discerned and understood by those with supernatural eyesight and ability to discern the spirits!

Obey God at any cost! Our God is a Super Natural Being. He operates only in the supernatural realm! We are now living in a season of Super Natural increased activities. Pay attention to our weather patterns. How they have changed. Earthquakes in divers places (i.e. Arlington, Texas). Extreme cold in the deep south (Atlanta, Georgia) hot lands. Unpredicted snow and ice storms... Pay attention to our safety. They too have changed. Elementary school shootings. Most recently, the stabbing in a Pennsylvania school. Military men being shot and killed by fellow soldiers at home (on post). Unbelievable! To fight in war — then come home and die — in what is believed to be a safe place.

Chapter I.

A Highway to Heaven

While flying back home to the United States of America from London and Southern, England, I met a gentle man on the plane. His name was Bob.

I was returning from a very inspirational, productive, evangelistic trip. Bob was seated next to me. He asked me what I do for a living, and why I happened to be on this flight. As I answered his questions, the door was opened for me to talk about My Lord and to tell of His Super Natural Power.

The nature of this conversation catapulted me into sharing with Bob about My Supernatural Experience with Death. Bob listened intently to my story. Afterwards, he took a deep breath and upon exhaling, he replied, Have you put your testimony in a book yet? No, I replied. Why not? He asked! Then he said, People need to hear about this kind of Miracle. I said, Yes! I know they do. I will publish my story for His Glory!

Many months later, I had procrastinated writing. My testimony had not been written, yet. Just then the Holy

Spirit reminded me again, "You must publish your story, Now! Others need to hear, and to be encouraged. Their faith needs to increase. Remember that, 'Faith comes by hearing...' Time is running out, Jesus is on His way back Soon! Tell my people to get ready, be ready and stay ready!"

And immediately afterward, my Lord gave me this mandate. He said, "Write and complete your writing. Start March 1 and complete it in March." This mandate was given to me so that I would stop procrastinating and walk in obedience. I know that disobedience will cause God's promises and favor to be null and void! Is that what you and I want? No, No, No! **Stop procrastinating and do your God given assignment. Get into the flow, obey God and live!**

Discernment

Discern the Spirits. Do not allow disruption, distraction, delay — watch and pray in the Spirit. There will be many, many other things that will try to interfere with your God given assignment. They appear to show themselves to be more important and more rewarding than the Lords mandate. The Holy Spirit has already given the orders, clearly. Be obedient and get your work done.

As I walked in obedience, my Lord, God would not let these "little foxes" spoil the vine. Nor to hinder His work. Obedience and faith is the key that unlocks the door to the supernatural. Favor turns the key and locks it into blessings, miracles and favor. Peter said, "We must obey God, rather than man." [Acts 5:29]

Don't Stop

Nehemiah was busy rebuilding the broken down wall around Jerusalem. He would not come down from the wall, as Sanballot and his crew wanted him to do. He said, "I can't come down from this wall — I am doing a great work and I cannot come down from this wall. Why should the work stop while I leave it and come down to you?"

You may never have been tempted by your enemy, or through other people to stop your God-given assignment, and come down and join them. I have! Be aware, when you are tempted. Resist satan, and he will flee from you. You must not let satan delay, discourage or destroy you.

Chapter II.

Changing Drivers

Janie had driven all night in route to Los Angeles, California. About 9:00 or 9:30 a.m. she had become very weary and decided to stop at a roadside park. It is my time to drive now, I said to Janie. It was before 10:00 am, a beautiful, sun shiny day. Not a cloud to be found in the West, Texas sky.

Janie had pulled over into a place to rest. There were no trees or shade to be found. The temperature had already climbed to near 100 degrees and the hot Texas sun was beaming down on us, as we sat in her van. She needed rest. I could not rest. Trying to rest, I said to Janie, "I can't get comfortable at all while sitting here. Why can't we keep rolling? Every minute and every mile counts! We still have a lot of miles ahead of us. There is a long, long road ahead or us."

Reluctantly, she agreed to let me drive while she rested her eyes for a short time! Was this the worse decision? A good idea or a God idea... or was it the best decision? It was all in God's plan, somehow. [Romans 8:28]

I had only driven approximately 20 minutes before the Big Bang. A supernatural, deadly crash, that turned into My Supernatural road trip to Heaven! instead of a Los Angeles, California trip to help the needy.

Narrative Report:

On June 10, Alva's vehicle struck road construction equipment and machinery negligently operating in her lane of traffic. The equipment and machinery was owned and operated by defendants, Holes Inc.

The above described accident occurred at a location identified as 9 miles W. of the City of Conway, Texas, on 1-40, 100 FT W. of Mile Post #88, Carson County, State of Texas, all was more fully set forth on an accident report obtained from Accident Records, Texas Department of Public Safety, #6113436.

As a direct and proximate result of said action by the equipment operators, Janie Fulmer and Alva Wilson suffered severe injuries including injuries to their neck and back, sever pain and mental anguish, and both have lost time from their employment and school."

The following is a Narrative Report, concerning the injuries of Ms. Wilson, which were sustained as a result of an auto accident on June 10 at approximately 9:30 in the morning.

HISTORY:

Ms. Wilson was examined and began treatments. She reported being involved in an auto accident,. She sustained injuries primarily to the neck, upper back, shoulders and mid back. Secondary type injuries were noted in the low back and pelvic region. The patient reported she was the driver of the vehicle when it was struck.

There was a large yellow piece of equipment with an extended ladder. It extended approximately three feet over an improperly yellow marked line. The equipment was close to the lane of on-coming traffic. It was very difficult to see this ladder. She observed there should have been more warning signs for drivers to see. Consequently, the mirror of her van struck the ladder. The mirror exploded and broke the entire window of the van. Glass shattered all over the front seat, floor, and down each side of the vehicle.

A flying object struck me in the forehead. I heard a loud bang. It was like the sound of a shotgun blast. Everything in my world blacked out. I thought I had been shot in the head. Somehow, I knew I had lost consciousness. I could no longer control my vehicle. I knew it was time to call for help. Finally, I called to Janie saying "Janie, come up here, I need you". After further discussion with Janie, she indicated I had never said anything to her. That's when the Supernatural power of God took control.

Chapter III.

During the Big Bang

During the accident, my spirit left my body. By this, I'm telling you, there was a separation of spirit, soul and body. My natural body, this outer shell, flesh, blood, bones and skin stayed in the van. Meanwhile, my inner-parts (invisible), spirit and soul was lifted up to Heaven. That part of me spent time in the precious presence of my Lord.

My spirit was looking down on my body, as one looks in a mirror to see what he looks like. I could see the reflection of myself. I had a laceration on my forehead and blood dripping down my face.

This reminded me of a childhood incident that was similar in nature. As a child, I was the victim of an unfortunate accident also. I am wearing a scar from two boys fighting on our way from school one day. The big 200-pound guy was fighting a much smaller boy. The little boy broke free and ran pass me just as the big guy threw a beer bottle to hit the little kid. He was running for his life; I got caught between the "devil and the deep blue sea!" Someone else who was walking behind me, yelled, "Watch out, Alva." I turned and looked back to see what was happening. That's when the mouth of that beer bottle struck me on the right side of my forehead.

Again, I was an innocent bystander and victim. However, I was delivered from victim to victory. It just happened to be a few yards away from the home of a nurse. She took care of my bleeding, wounded, hurting head. My 2 older brothers walked me home. We lived 10 miles out in the country. No one out there had a telephone yet! Neither did we have ready access to a doctor. But God! He has supernaturally kept me all of my life, and He is still keeping me!

No Entrance — Do Not Enter

You Can't Come In — The Promise

While all of this sin activity was being displayed on Interstate 40, I was talking to my Lord. I stood at the Pearly Gates while He was talking to me. You can't come in! These words were not comforting, but rather confusing. What did you say, my Lord? What do you mean, I can't come in? Immediately I went into denial. He could not have said that, I can't come in? Okay, did I really hear Him correctly? I was absolutely stunned. After that, I felt disappointed. I was totally discombobulated. My question was, "Why? Why? Why, my Lord, why can't I come in?" The haunting sound was resonating in my spirit.

I knew that I had always loved my Lord! Even as a child, I had confessed Jesus Christ as my Lord and Savior. I have always delighted in serving Him. I lived for Jesus, my entire life. I have never been a back-slider. I did not say, I had never sinned. I have sinned, and so have you!

My Sin's Washed Away

But I knew I was forgiven. You may ask, How can you be so sure? I'm glad you asked. Because I confessed my sins, and you must too, accept Jesus! Only then, can you be sure of Heaven!

As a child, I confessed Jesus Christ as my Lord and Savior. I communed with Him daily and followed Him in water Baptism. As an adult, I was baptized in the Jordan River in Israel. I have faith in my Lord and His Holy Word. Therefore, I could not miss Heaven, and neither can you. We MUST follow the red letters in the New Testament which tells us to confess Jesus and repent of our sin. You can be sure of your salvation. Be Obedient! "Salvation is not of works, lest any man should boast"... but it's because of His grace and mercy by the Blood of Jesus. (Ephesians 2:8-9).

You Must go Back

During Spirit talk two — I said, "No, I do not want to go back. I want to stay here with you. Then I asked Him, why? What is it Lord... again I said, I want to stay here!" After a brief pause, there was total silence. My Lord said to me, "Your work is not finished on earth! You must go back for Mama and Tony." My birth mother is Mama and Tony is my youngest son. I love both of them dearly. When my Lord said, "for Mama and Tony" He touched my heart's soft spot. It was then that I accepted His command. I relaxed and said, "Yes my Lord, I will go back." He replied, Mama needs you to take care of her. If you will obey my instructions you will never, ever lack for any good thing. I will meet your every need.

Spirit talk three — about Mom

This promise includes rest. Provision of daily needs, long life, good health, happiness, peace and joy! Your work is not finished on Earth. Jesus reveals more about Mom. Take care of Mama until I call her home to be with Me. Mama has served Me well. She has served her family faithfully, and very well all of her lifetime. Keep her in a dignified manner. Keep her clean, well dressed, in a lovely clean home environment, as you have already done! Do not place her in a nursing home that would not meet her classy, clean living standards. Keep her living standards high as you have already done for her. As you continue to bless Mama, I will keep on blessing you, tremendously!

Chapter IV.

No Fear Here
Fear Not

Nothing was wrong. Before my experience with death, I was so sure of my salvation. Here, my name was being called every time the word **salva**tion was used. How neat is that? What Blessed Assurance, Jesus is Mine! I'm an heir of salvation, purchased by God. Born of His Spirit — washed in His blood! It does not get any better than that. I did not fear or doubt for a moment that I was going to hell! I simply, just did not understand why His command: and what He meant! Nothing was wrong. It was simply not my time. I had arrived home too early. I guess my guardian angel forgot to re-set my clock. He remembered to "spring forward", but forgot to Fall back. Therefore, the time changed and I arrived too early. It was not my appointed time, yet! Consequently, I had to return back to earth — complete my assignment and wait on the Lord's timing.

As I stood in His presence, there was no thought of time or any worldly thing — just the Holy presence of my Lord.

I don't know how much time we spent together! All I really know is that overwhelming Peace rested upon me and covered me like a warm cozy blanket on a cold winter night!

However, those stunning words, "You can't come in" were devastating. Until I heard all of his orders and why? And understood all of his commands, clearly (your work is not finished), then I was ready to obey and carry on His plan. I knew, I would enter in at the correct time. But not now — my assignment was not complete.

Chapter V.

Who Controlled and Stopped the Van? An Invisible Man

Immediately after the van struck the big yellow machine that was obstructing the road, I lost total control. I was not conscious of any activity surrounding me. I went instantly into the precious presence of my Lord.

The van went out of my control and into the control of the Holy Spirit. The worker with Hole Inc. gave his account of what he saw. "The van rolled and wobbled down 1-40. It rocked from side to side". It appeared to him that we were sure to roll completely over on our side at any minute and crash. However, the vehicle would set back up straight again, as if some thing would catch it, and tilt it back upon its wheels before tumbling over. The van would rock, roll and wobble straight down the highway. This activity continued on for three to five miles down Interstate 40, finally coming to a road side park. The vehicle, supernaturally exited off the road, into this park, and came to a complete stop!!!

Chapter VI.

The Flaming Torch
The First Night After the Accident:

After the doctor examined and released us from the hospital, we found a hotel room to rest. Our attending physician prescribed tranquilizers for Janie and me. He recommended complete bed rest for both of us.

However, that first night, as we were resting in our hotel room — a strange supernatural occurrence happened. Our sleep was suddenly interrupted. Both, Janie and I heard this noise. It woke us up. Both of us sat straight up in our separate beds, at the same time. We looked at one another — then there was a moment of complete silence — we were so startled. Then I spoke and said, "Janie did you hear something?" She said, "Yes, I did. Did you?" I replied, "Yes, I did too!" So, what did you hear, Alva? I said, "I heard something that sounded like glass breaking or keys rattling. I thought that someone was trying to get into our room." She said, "I did too!"

What I Saw

Next I saw, with supernatural eyesight, a Big Angel standing between our beds. This supernatural being was dressed in a long white robe trimmed with gold. The angel had large widespread wings, which hovered over both beds. His wings appeared to be gentle, lifting up and down over us as a protective covering. (for He will give His angels charge over thee... Psalms 91:1 (KJV).. We took refuge in the shelter of His wings, where we were absolutely secure.

The angel left us, and immediately my Lord walked in and came to me, handed me a torch and said, "Run with this torch." Tell everyone you see to get ready and stay ready to meet Me, Jesus! I am coming soon! No on knows the time nor the hour." We do not know the exact time. He does give us a clue. Watch for the season!

The Spirit of My Lord gave me this torch and said, "Run with it!"

Chapter VII.

The Two Intercessors

*A*s soon as the van came to a standstill in the park, we were greeted by two people, a husband and wife. They were intercessors sent by God. It appeared as if they were sent to the park to meet our needs. They were at the right time and in the right place to pray, pray, pray... "They shall lay hands on the sick and they (the sick) shall recover." (Mark 16:18c) KJV

The husband secured our broken window so that we could safely travel and find someone to make repairs.

After getting me out of the van, and rescuing Jane, they prayed for us. Janie feeling trapped in the back of her van, was yelling hysterically, "Get me out of here! Get me out of here!"

In a "tongue and cheek fashion" I made this statement, earlier on as Janie crawled into the back of her luxury van to rest I said, "I am locking you in for safe keeping while I drive." I had no idea of Janie not being safe, and rested. Look at what happened...

I have an excellent driving record. Since Janie had driven all night long, I thought certainly, I can drive on this beautiful, sunny day — no problem, while she rested.

God's Super Natural Intervention

Two Nurses & A Cell Phone

Remember this was before the popularity of the cell phone. There was not, even a telephone booth at this park, but God... Provided.

Two nurses just happened to be parked at the same roadside park. They had a cell phone to call for help. The state troopers and ambulances came quickly.

Remember the old phone booths? We don't see them any more. The cell phone was a thing of the future, a luxury, that only the rich and the famous could afford. Only doctors, nurses and successful business men had them. Neither Janie or I had a cell phone at that time. We were not rich or famous!

The Two Intercessors

Do you see the super natural hand of God in this? Some people would say, "oh they were so lucky — NO! This is not luck. It is the super natural power of God. He is at work in your life and mine today. Favor, grace and His mercy re-wrote my life.

God's Sovereign Power

God put the nurses and intercessors at that exact place for us! Hallelujah!!! He knew just where we would be. He knew this accident was going to happen before we left home. You may say, "Well, since God knows everything, why would He allow this accident to happen?" He could have prevented this. You may also say,. "You were going to do a good work, a much needed work, for the Lord. . Helping the poor. Why, why, why. I just don't understand".

You may also argue, "But God is Sovereign. He can do what he wants and we will come out on top, victoriously! "He's a Sovereign God.". Just remember, He said in Romans 8:28 (KJV) that "all things work together for the good of those who love Him..."

Why did Paul ignore the warning in Acts 21 (KJV)? He was warned not to go on the missionary journey on his way to Jerusalem. They were told what would happen. I recalled what Janie told me. She said that John (her husband) did not totally agree with her traveling on this trip, but she knew to go by grace. God had a plan back then on June 10. His purpose was being revealed today in the publishing of this book. Do you think God knows what time it is? Well, He does know!

It is our responsibility to just accept God's command and obey Him! In Acts 21 (KJV), Paul was warned not to go to Jerusalem. But this was God's plan for him. Therefore he went ahead and accepted the pain and suffering for God's glory. But, he had to obey God's plan for his life. Acts 21:14 (KJV) says, "so when he would not be persuaded, we ceased, saying, the will of the Lord be done."

Paul's warning on the journey to Jerusalem in Acts 21:4 (KJV),....and finding disciples, we tarred there seven days. "They told Paul through the Spirit, not to go up to Jerusalem." But he did not obey them. But rather, obeyed God Acts 21:5b (KJV) "and we kneeled down on the shore, and prayed." (King James Version)

Chapter VIII.

The State Trooper Investigates

The State Troopers came to investigate the cause of the accident and determine who was at fault. They questioned me, at the beginning, but I was too incoherent to give the straight of it! Therefore, Janie took charge and started to tell her version of what happened.

One of the officers yelled at her and said, "Shut up woman! How do you know the details of how this all happened? Weren't you in the back of your van sleeping?" Yes, she replied, but I do know what happened. The State Trooper said, "Well, we will all soon know the truth in just a few minutes, whether you know or not!" The Holy Spirit speaks to Janie. "We are going back to the scene of the accident, and interview the workers there." Okay, she said! You will see, I do know! Janie was getting upset because they would not listen to her. I heard the trembling in her voice.

The Holy Spirit speaks again explicitly, "Do not leave Janie here alone!" I did not go to the hospital by ambulance. Obey God! Janie was too shaken up to be left alone after the accident. She was in a strange place, a long, long way from home. She was not too coherent and should not be left alone. Her husband, John, was at least fourteen hours away. We needed to stick together! The Holy Spirit prompted me to stay by her side! And I obeyed. I did not go to the hospital with the paramedics. Therefore, I had to sign a release for the ambulance driver that would release them from any liabilities.

The State Troopers return to the park. I was lying down on a picnic table, covered with a blanket. He said (as his finger pointed upward toward Heaven), someone is up there watching over you. You should be dead." I wanted to say to him, "Sir, I was dead until Jesus breathed the breath of life back into my lifeless body. However, it was obvious they were already in a state of confusion. It was quite difficult for them to grasp how Janie knew all the details of the accident. She knew everything, even though she was asleep in the back of her van . It was even more confusing that the driver, Alva, is revealing that she was dead, but alive now! Wow! It's supernatural.

Before we could leave the park the State Troopers had to finish their report. The State Troopers went to the site, then returned back to give us their findings. They were absolutely speechless, dumbfounded, with one question to ask Janie. "How did you know what happened. How could you know? The witnesses gave us the same report as you, almost verbatim, word for word." Janie and I,knew why. It's supernatural!

Sometime later after the State Troopers finished their report, we finally left the park. Immediately after the crash, I was in shock, feeling tired and sleepy. I was trying to return into that heavenly place where there was peace and no pain. I could not go back there. I was dizzy, in pain, itching, my head ached, confused and fearful, wondering what would happen next.

Janie worked and worked trying to clean all the glass from her van before leaving the park, but that was impossible! The van was in drivable condition. Consequently, Janie was able to drive us to the nearest hospital. We finally left the park, arrived at the hospital. The nurses and attendants on duty looked at me and said, "Oh my, she is glittering like a downtown Christmas tree!" There was so much glass covering me from head to toe! I was glittering, burning and itching. The nurses said to me, they wished they could do more to relieve my discomfort. However, the only instruction was to stand under warm running water. I was also advised as the water flows, do not rub or scratch, but let the running water do its work. Have you ever been itching and could not scratch? It is very irritating and aggravating. If I were to rub or scratch, I would do more permanent damage to my skin. I did not want that to happen.

Chapter IX.

Obedience — The Only Way to Go
A Miracle In St. Louis

We rested and slept until we again felt like driving. We ate a small snack, prayed and Janie was ready to drive. From the hotel, Janie drove us back to St. Louis, where my sister, Maxie, lives. She made us welcome to stay over, as long as we needed to stay. In the meantime, we had heard about a Healing Revival. Rodney Howard Brown would be the featured speaker. We knew we should attend. This was another miraculous provision that my Lord had set up for us.

As we stepped into the foyer of the church, miracles started to happen. At the time of altar call, Janie and I pushed our way through the crowd. Hands were laid on us and we were slain in the Spirit. As I rose up from that anointed floor, all of the glass which entered by body as a result of the accident was gone! There was no glass, no pain and no itching! Hallelujah, it was Supernaturally removed! That night, Janie and I spent our time rejoicing with my sister, Maxie!

The next day we left St. Louis and headed to Tulsa. We spent some time there and visited Oral Roberts University (ORU) and the anointed prayer tower. This is the landmark that Dr. Oral Roberts built and prayed for thousands. I praise God for Great Generals of God's Army, like Dr. Oral Roberts and others.

Meanwhile, everywhere we stopped, we told others about the Love of Jesus and invited them to be sure, to be ready when He comes. We kept the Flaming Torch moving.

We were finally back home to Indiana. Janie's husband, John, was so relieved when he saw her. He was happy to see that she was all in one piece after such a horrific accident! He took the van to the garage and had it fixed. Soon it was ready to drive to our next evangelistic trip.

Chapter X.

Satan's Ploy to Destroy Me Uncovered

Satan's ploy was to destroy me. I was studying for my degree in Drug & Alcohol Addiction Counseling. Satan's tactic was to get me out of the race. I was already counseling people and getting them set free from all types of demonic oppression and depression. You see, I knew what to do with my B.A. Degree — "Born Again Degree." I was studying and being mentored by the world's greatest demon destroying man of God, Dr. Lester Sumerall. Thank God for this General who was tough and loved by many.

Satan's Plan

Satan intended first to kill me in the car accident. However, he missed his target. God had me covered by the Blood of Jesus! Hallelujah! Since he could not kill me there, he thought he had a better trick! His intention was to get me addicted on prescription drugs. My doctor had prescribed Valium for me. It is definitely a drug that many have gotten addicted to. The enemies attempt was to get me in the position where I would need a drug counselor. But God! Mercy said, no, I'm not going to let her go.

I set an appointment to see a counselor because I was in so much pain. I needed some help to cope with the mental and physical agony I was experiencing. I told the counselor that the pain bothers me all the time. I was having trouble with my upper left shoulder area and at the base of my neck. I was enduring mental blocks and lapses. I was a candidate for depression.

I had difficulty sleeping and significant disruptions in my every day life patterns. I lost interest in things and had an increase worry and anxiety, frequent bouts of crying, discouragement, and flashbacks of the accident. All of these were symptoms resulting from the big bang accident. Satan tried unsuccessfully to take my life.

When I spoke with this counselor, I needed him to let me know the status of my condition. I was wondering how much better I will get. I knew that God was with me and I would get better. I was not sure when or how it would happen. I was not angry at God that this happened. But, I felt very sad that the accident occurred. I acknowledged that the overall experience was a terrible psychological trauma. Yet, there was also a spiritual element which was very positive. I told the counselor that the angels were there that day. I went to a peaceful place and had a conversation with God. God told me that I had to go back for my mother and son.

I further explained to the counselor that I had some increased tension and discomfort around people. This was especially the case when I was called upon to interact. It's amazing, but during this time in my life, I had many people calling and requesting prayer and counseling for themselves. It was almost unbearable, because I needed so much prayer and counseling for myself. My thoughts were "how could I even begin to help others with their plights and unfortunate conditions?" I had to trust, pray and have faith in God to see me through!

One faithful day, I was shaking and trembling as a result of the accident. My dearest friend, Tina, a seasoned intercessor and Mighty Woman of God called me. "Hello, Alva,", she said. "How are you doing?" Not very well at this time, I said, I'm very nervous. She started to pray (in the Holy Spirit) for me. When she finished, I said, I'm better. Next she said, "now lay that phone receiver down, go throw that valium down the toilet, flush it and come back to the phone. I was obedient. I did exactly what she told me to do. She saw Satan's plan for me. That instant, as she prayed, and I obeyed, the devil lost his hold on me. Praise God I am free! I started going to a Christian counselor, Dr. King, who worked with Natural Medicines. Dr. King used Orthomolecular Therapy and monitored closely my depression and lack of sleep. I'm so glad I obeyed. I no longer needed tranquilizers or anti depressants. I'm free!

Satan's Plan Destroyed

Not every situation will be a quick process. Some things take longer and lots of patience and labor. This Orthomolecular Therapy was long and laborious. However, with the help of my doctors, therapist, prayers of the saints and our healer, my Lord and Savior, Jesus Christ, we got the victory. Again, we overcame Satan by the Blood of the Lamb and the Word of our testimony! We are continually moving from Victim to Victory! Amen!

The latest, greatest supernatural miracle of all is this: I can write. I am using my right hand again. On May 11, 2013, I had a stroke. My right side was totally out of commission. I could hardly hold a pen or pencil in my hand. I could not sign my name. I could not write out my wants or to do a grocery list. I could not reach for an object (e.g. glass of water) or anything. As I would reach for an object, I would miss it by two inches or more. My perception was off and I had lost total control of my hand. It would not go where I was trying to send it! But God!!

I have handwritten every page of this book before having it typed. I could have used my little digital tape recorder, but I wanted to show ole-slew-foot, the devil, he can't keep a good, faithful, hard working, praying woman down! I am writing more legible than before the stroke. I am doing all of my housework, driving my car, cooking and now living alone in beautiful Rockwall, Texas. Praise God!

Devil's Work – Supernatural Too (The Deception)

Don't be fooled by the "source" from which the supernatural comes! An example of this is found in the Book of Acts. Acts 16:16-18 (KJV) is as follows:

> **16)** *And it came to pass, as we went to prayer, a certain damsel possessed with a spirit of divination met us, which brought her masters much gain by soothsaying:* **17)** *The same followed Paul and us, and cried, saying, These men are the servants of the most high God, which shew unto us the way of salvation.* **18)** *And this did she many days. But Paul, being*

grieved, turned and said to the spirit, I command thee in the name of Jesus Christ to come out of her. And he came out the same hour.

The woman in these scriptures were following God's disciples saying "these men are men of God, listen to them!" Yet, she was full of the devil. Her voice was a distraction to what was being said, but she was saying "the truth"! She was creating a scene. She was also drawing attention to herself while distracting from God's Spirit and His Word spoken through the disciples.

The Apostle Paul discerned (gift of discernment given to Him by the Holy Spirit) that evil spirit controlling the woman. He commanded it to "release" the woman in the Name of Jesus Christ. Every believer gets their Authority in Jesus' Name. By the Name of Jesus every evil spirit has to obey. The woman was delivered from that evil spirit which was causing her to react as if the Holy Spirit was controlling her. I call that kind of behavior, deception.

My analogy of this story can be compared to preparing a meal. To get started one must have the necessary cooking utensils. You must make sure they are clean and ready to use. The pots, pans or utensils that one uses need to be cleaned otherwise the food prepared in them will be contaminated. By this same token, the woman was saying all the right words, yet she was controlled by an unclean spirit. Therefore, what came out of her mouth was impure (not clean). Before God can successfully use anyone, he or she must be clean.

Satan is an imitation of God and His Holy Spirit! He has no thoughts of his own. He only tries to imitate the True and

Living God! He is a deceiver. 2 Corinthians 11:14 (KJV) .....for even Satan disguises himself as an angel of light.)

Do you have enough of God's anointing in you to know the difference? Take a look at the scripture in Acts 4:7-10: (KJV)

> *And when they had set them in the midst, they asked, By what power, or by what name, have ye done this?* ***8)*** *Then Peter, filled with the Holy Ghost, said unto them, Ye rulers of the people, and elders of Israel,* ***9)*** *If we this day be examined of the good deed done to the impotent man, by what means he is made whole;* ***10)*** *Be it known unto you all, and to all the people of Israel, that by the name of Jesus Christ of Nazareth, whom ye crucified, whom God raised from the dead, even by him doth this man stand here before you whole.*

Here again, we see that believers in Jesus Christ of Nazareth are given Authority over evil spirits. In Jesus' name they MUST obey!

Chapter XI.

Back to School

I missed only two days of school. I attended classes while in excruciating pain. Therefore, I had to take drugs (i.e., prescribed drugs). They can be harmful and very addictive. Also, many patients get hooked on prescribed drugs. They are as harmful to the body as the street drugs if you are not careful while taking them, and the results from prescribed drugs cause the person to react as though the drug they are addicted to is a street drug. It does not matter — Prescription or Street drug — the results are the same if one gets addicted to them.

Earlier in this book, you read how I escaped from this deadly addiction. The pain medication that was prescribed for me caused drowsiness. I could not stay awake in class. Therefore, I took two pillows to my classroom. One pillow was to sit on, the other was to place on my desk and rest my head.

Among other aids, I took a small tape recorder to record all lectures. I would go home and listen to the lectures, over and over until I could remember and memorize the most important parts, something that may be on a test or final exam. Missing too many classes was automatic failure. I could not take the chance and miss classes. Therefore, by taking my comfort aids, such as the pillows and also recording my classes, I could not be counted as absent. I was present, with pain medication, my pillow and whatever I found to bring comfort.

I graduated, by the grace of God, with patience, pushing and pulling, prayer and persistence. I was sprinkled and marinated with lots of favor from God and man. I was able to take all of my final exams, do my practicum (assigned lessons) and squeeze in an extra class. I did not know I should not have taken the extra class. The University did not approve of an overload of courses. Consequently, I took a class that would not have been approved. The officials did not know that I was enrolled in the class. It was final exam day and I had two exams scheduled at the same hour. The only way I could do both was to take the first exam, finish it quickly, then ask my professor if I may be excused to go take the other exam.

When I approached him with my request, he answered no. He said you can't do that. I asked him, why not? He said because it's considered too much of a load by the University rules. I said to him, I've already finished the class. I further told him all I needed was his permission to be dismissed in order to go to take the other exam. He looked at me in total disbelief. How did you do that? He asked. Then he took my hand and said, "let's pray." He dismissed me. I was able to take my final exam.

My Lord blessed me to make good grades. I graduated within the two year time span. PRAISE THE LORD! You may ask why was there a mandate to graduate within two years. I was given the two-year time span because the degree program for the Bachelor of Science in Alcohol and Drug Abuse Counseling, BSADC was to be a closed opportunity. It was scheduled to end after the summer of 1997 and would not be offered again. It was scheduled to end after that summer and would not be offered again. Had I attended school after the summer, I would have missed my Divine opportunity to receive my B.S. Degree from Indiana Wesleyan University. Thank God, I was willing and did obey His instructions.

Chapter XII.

Where Is Tony?

As for Tony, he is alive and well today, by a very astonishing move of God on March 1, 2014. About midnight, Tony was driving around the majestic mountainside of West, Virginia, when his twenty-five ton load of round steel pipes shifted. The truck swayed and shifted, he loss control and hit a guard rail. Tons of steel pipes rolled down the mountainside, cutting a trail of trees down and kicking up dirt like a bulldozer. The steel pipes rolled down the mountainside. They crossed over another road beneath the highway he was traveling and finally came to a stop. Supernaturally, no one was driving along that lower mountainside. There were no houses on the road. Had there been, the people in those homes would have been crushed to death. Miraculously, not a person was touched.

One man driving along behind him, was an eye witness to the entire Miracle. He was not affected by the accident. The witness stated that he hit and ran over something, but kept right on going. Tony says, it was his tarp, the cover for his load of steel. He was not injured. No injuries and the truck was still drive-able. Now! That's Supernatural!!! (Psalms 91)

As for Tony, "He must answer my call on his life and walk faithfully in it," saith God! "Oh, yes! Alva there are many others that you will minister to, and they shall be mine," saith the Lord. "Sanctified, Saved and Delivered, as you run, run, run, with the torch, my anointed Word, as an Olympic runner runs with the torch and passes it on to the next runner. So will you."

Here is what God said to me:

> *"Tony and Mama are your assignment, Alva, saith God. Do not drop the torch, but rather pass it on. Teach them to tell the lost and dying world, I AM COMING and I am coming soon. Prepare to meet Jesus and stay ready, He said. You will not have more time to get ready when I come for you. It will be too late. Behold, I am coming quickly and my reward is with me. In the twinkling of an eye, I shall return for you. No one knows the time, hour or season, not even Jesus. Only God knows."*

Tony was involved in the truck accident and his life and the life of others were spared. He and others have a chance to get ready, if they will hearken to the voice of my Lord. Yet, I was involved in the car accident, and there was no more time to get ready. Immediately, I was in another world, standing before the Lord!

Chapter XIII.

What Happened With Mama?

The Holy Spirit spoke to me saying, "Take good care of your mother in a very dignified manner. Obey me and you will never lack or need for anything or anyone to take good care of you. You reap what you sow."

At the age of forty-two, Mom Oliver had an aneurysm at home. My dad, the late Rev. M.L. Oliver, was away at church. I was with him about an hours drive from home at Bosqueville Baptist Church, where he was pastor. We did not have cell phones back then. My sister-in-law, Reva, was home with mom when it happened. My dad received the word, through one of his church members that mom was very ill and we needed to get home quickly.

When we arrived home on Highway 6 in Harrison Switch, we found mama in severe pain, headache and at the point of death. We placed her in the car and we sped away back to Waco. I was driving the car as we headed to the hospital. The doctors finally examined her and she was admitted into Providence Hospital. Their findings were not good. Mom had an aneurysm, a vein burst in her head, blood was dripping onto her brain and surgery was absolutely necessary to try to save her life. The doctors told us that mom would never be well again, if she lived through the night. They said she would be lifeless, like a vegetable, no movement or control of her body.

Now, my dad, a great man of faith said to the doctors, "go ahead and try the surgery." The doctor said, "I'll do my best, but nothing is certain to work." The doctor was going to operate on mom the following morning. However, he postponed surgery until the second day after mom was admitted to the hospital! On the second day the doctor decided he still could not do the surgery. On the third day, victory! No surgery was needed! My dad had stayed by mom's bedside all night praying. mom told the story of her healing like this:

She said, "dad had prayed and cried all night long, pleading her case before Jesus, to let her live — He (dad) needed her and her nine living children needed her." We ranged in ages twenty years old down to two years of age. I was sixteen at the time. I was praying fervently, too, because I did not want to take her position as mom, at such an early age. Not only that, I loved her and we children needed her desperately.

Mom told me that "she gave up and did not want to live. But dad pleaded with her, praying, don't leave me."

What took place on the third day: A Supernatural Miracle

Mom was lying there in bed wanting to go on and be with Jesus. She felt so sorry for dad as he had been on his knees all night long, pleading for her health. She reached her hand over to comfort and console him, and patted him on the head, but as she was trying to touch him, she felt a big wet spot in her bed! Dampness was all the way under her back, as if she had urinated in her bed. But she knew, she had not done that! As she struggled to touch him and make some sense of the wet bed — she soon realized that the wetness was dads tears. He had cried a bucket of tears. The anointing from his tears touched her hand and soared into her body — at that very moment, she was instantly, Supernaturally Healed! He jumped up from his knees and she jumped out of her bed of affliction and they started doing the "Holy Dance," something they did not do as Baptist. They were dancing and speaking in tongues. (Acts 10:46)

Mom's roommate witnessed all of this commotion, as mom and dad danced and shouted. Mom was shouting, "I'm Healed! I'm Healed! I'm Healed!" The nurses came running into the room, shouting at my dad in anger and fear, "Get out of here! What are you trying to do, kill her? Get out, get out now!" Mom was yelling at the nurses as they were throwing dad out of the room and assisting mom back into her hospital bed. "I'm healed, please don't take me into the OR", she cried. Things finally calmed down. Mom was back in bed and dad was outside the room Praising God! Doctors and nurses were in a state of unbelief. The nurses said, "Okay, okay, we will see how healed you are. In just a few minutes, you are going back to x-ray. We will see!"

Mom begged the nursing staff, "please don't take me to the OR! I am healed!" The x-ray proved – she was totally healed. At that time, she was forty-two years old. Providence Hospital dismissed her and she walked out very alive and well. It was a demonstration of God's Supernatural Healing Power!

She remains healed. Mom went to Heaven on March 5, 2012 at 5:30 p.m. She received TOTAL HEALING and was never sick, ever again. "By His stripes, we are healed.....we were healed...." (Isaiah 53:5, 1 Peter 2:24)

Chapter XIV.

The Long Journey to Complete Healing

Upon arrival back home, we started our therapy and doctor's appointments. This would be a long road back to total healing – except there be another super natural healing....and it did prove to be a miracle.

My Faith

My faith in God's Healing Power carried me on back into classes and graduation! How I managed to stay in school, graduate on time – with my other class members is due to my faith in God. We started and finished together.

The enemy wanted me to give up and not graduate on time. You see, God had already told me that I must graduate within a two year time span. One day the Holy Spirit had spoken destiny to me...I knew that and I made sure I obeyed His instructions. I found out that the program degree which I pursued would not be offered at the university the next year. I was a member of the last graduating class. If I had not obeyed – I would have missed graduating. Some of my classmates were whispering behind my back, saying, "She's not going to graduate! She's not going to make it!" Amazingly, I did, and some of the gossipers and naysayers did not make it. "The **heart is** deceitful above all things, and **desperately wicked**: who can know it?" (Jeremiah 17:9 KJV) Sometimes you must be careful with the words you speak for "death and life are in the power of the tongue." (Proverbs 18:21a KJV) Another scripture which comes to mind is found in Proverbs 15:4 – A gentle **tongue** [with its healing power] **is** a tree of life, but willful contrariness in it breaks down the spirit." (Amplified Bible) I know this was a Supernatural move of God and obedience on my part! PRAISE THE LORD!

Dear readers, be very careful what you say. It may "boomerang" on you and stop your progress – and not the person you are speaking about!!! We win if we don't quit.

Have the Faith of God

In this natural world, as we know it, I never received the extra credit hours, because I never arrived at the center in Los Angeles, California.

However, by God's grace and favor, supernaturally, I graduated on schedule. I walked across the stage at Indiana Wesleyan University in August 1997 and received my Bachelor of Science Degree in Alcohol & Drug Abuse Counseling (BSADC) in spite of the devil's attack on my life.

We win if we don't quit! A mustard seed size faith is all you need. And you know, I graduated with good grades despite everything I had encountered on this journey.

Chapter XV.

The Miracle of Moving — Living in Rockwall

A Miracle — God's Provision Approximately thirty years ago, Janie and I attended a conference in Houston, Texas. This meeting was so ordained by God, I was supposed to be there! However, I did not know I was supposed to be there. Janie had invited me to go with her. But, I was reluctant to go. Consequently, she drove from Indianapolis, Indiana to Houston, Texas... alone. About the second day, as she sat in the conference, the Holy Spirit said to her, "Alva needs to be here, drive back to Indianapolis and get her." On that day as we were driving through Rockwall I said, "Lord if I ever live in Texas again, I would like to live here in beautiful Rockwall. Accordingly, after mama died, I applied for an apartment in Rockwall and God worked a miracle. The process and waiting period was a test. However, I waited on my Lord, and He worked it out.

Early one morning in January I received a phone call telling me to come in **and** sign the lease on an apartment that was not my first choice. I agreed to come and sign, however, before I could get dressed and leave home. I received another phone call. It was the manager at the Rockwall apartments saying, "Ms. Alva, are you still interested in the apartment on our property?" Yes, yes, yes, I replied. "Well," she said, "I have two vacancies, you may have your one bedroom or two bedroom choice." Oh! What favor — I chose the one bedroom apartment.

I was living with friends in Fort Worth, Texas. Now, I needed furniture. I had given away and sold everything except Mom's lift chair, chest of drawers, table, and file cabinet.

Give

Luke 6:38 clearly speaks to God's people. It states, "Give and it shall be given unto you; good measure, pressed down, and shaken together, and running over, shall men give into your bosom. For with the same measure ye mete withal it shall be measured to you again." (Luke 6:38 KJV)

Proof

Several years ago, mom and I were moving to a Senior Citizen apartment. Therefore, we had to downsize. We had a garage full of lithographs which I needed to sell. Yet, I did not have the expertise on the marketing of these lithographs. Therefore, I had to get them out of that garage. I gave some of them to a lady. Somehow she moved out of state and I never heard another word from her.

The antique dining room is in the beautiful home of my daughter, Jackie. She takes good care of things, and makes good use of it. She and her husband are attorney's.

consequently, they do a lot of entertaining in their beautiful home. The Maccabean Dining Room Suit fits their lifestyle. However, I gave my Spiritual daughter some of my choice pieces of furniture, sold my china cabinet, and gave other pieces to a young newlywed couple.

The Miracle

My Spiritual daughter gave me back all that I had given her plus much, much more. And the newlyweds gave me back my china cabinet, coffee table, sofa and love seat, queen size mattresses and more. My pastor and church congregation gave me a "house warming" one Sunday afternoon. They completed my kitchen. All appliances are black and white — refrigerator, stove, and other kitchen items — dish towels and everything else I needed. Oh yes, my newlyweds and daughter, Cynthia, rented a truck and hauled the above mentioned furniture to my new place in Rockwall. The pastor and his wife filled my freezer with healthy foods, drinking water, cookware, dishes, etc.

Oh, you are so lucky, you may say. No, again I say, this is not luck. This is the super natural favor of God — let's call it what it is... Miracles, as a result of obedience.

The Move From Fort Worth to Rockwall

I knew that I needed help to make this move. However, the feeling in my heart kept saying to me, don't ask for help. This sounds crazy but the Lord told me. "Don't bother Keesha and Jeanette — my landlords and helpers, close friends who assist me on occasion." I knew they could move me as they have been my guardian angels each time that I had to move in times past. Oh, what life savers. Keesha and Jeanette have been to mama, down through the years. But the Spirit kept saying, "don't bother them." Keesha was having some trouble with her legs and feet and Jeanette is getting older. I was instructed not to ask my two brothers, who would have gladly moved me! Some people living in the Mesquite, Texas area, kept on asking me, "Sis. Alva who is going to move you?" All that I could say is "I don't know." Some of them probably thought I had lost my mind not making any arrangements to get help with this move. Oh yes, I was concerned about it, but not worried. My faith is in God! I knew he had a plan. But he had not revealed it to me.

The lesson was, that He was testing me to see if I had learned — "wait patiently on the Lord!" I passed! It had been a very cold night in Fort Worth. I slept on the couch in Keesha's living room with about 8 lbs. of blankets in an effort to keep warm. At about 11:00 am, I got up to use the bathroom. At the same time, Ebony, who is Keesha's daughter, was also headed to the bathroom. We greeted one another and I said, "Oh, I did not know you were here." She replied, "Yes, I'm not going to work today. She stated that Chris, her fiancé, and she were going to noon day prayer." I said, "Okay." In a few seconds the Holy Spirit spoke to me saying, "Why don't you go to prayer meeting too!" Therefore, I asked, "May I go with you? Sure," she said, "we will wait for you." I quickly got ready and off we were, headed to church. When we arrived at church, only two people were there. We joined in with them at the prayer meeting. We all prayed for approximately one hour. Then the leader called the meeting to an end.

God Answers "Who's going to move you?"

Just then she asked me the sixty-four dollar question, "Who is going to move you?" I said, "I don't know." She looked at me with a pleasant smile on her face and said, "Oh! My husband will move you, just give us a call and let us know when, where and what time you'll be ready to move." On Saturday morning, she and her husband and three little cute boys under six years of age, all came and moved me. Chris, Ebony's fiancé, also helped me move. This was the smoothest move I have ever made. I was concerned about my ability to do or help with the move because I had experienced a stroke less than a year ago. But God, He, will send help no matter how helpless your situation may look in the natural. Look to God, our provider. This season of my life was truly a Road Trip. I took a journey to Heaven and I wanted to stay, but God sent me back and I wouldn't change one thing. Through it all, God is the one who knows everything from beginning to the end. He is and will always be the Alpha and Omega!

The End.

Receive Jesus Christ as Lord and Savior of Your Life

The Bible says, "That if thou shalt confess with thy mouth the Lord Jesus Christ, and shalt believe in thine heart that God raised him from the dead, thou shalt be saved. For with the heart man believeth unto righteousness: and with the mouth confession is made unto salvation" (Romans 10:9,10).

To receive Jesus Christ as Lord and Savior of your life, sincerely pray this prayer from your heart.

Dear Jesus:

I believe that You died for me and that You rose again on the third day. I confess to You that I am a sinner and that I need Your love and forgiveness. Come into my life, forgive my sins, and give me eternal life. I confess you now as my Lord. Thank You for my salvation.

Write to us:
Alva Wilson Ministries/A Kingdom Builders Ministry,
P.O. Box 494986, Garland, TX 75049
Email: alvawilsonministries@yahoo.com
We will send you information to help you with your new life in Jesus Christ!

www.ingramcontent.com/pod-product-compliance
Lightning Source LLC
LaVergne TN
LVHW040257111125
825462LV00011B/599